A Purnell book
ISBN 0 361 03858 5
First published 1977. Reprinted 1987

Printed by Purnell Book Production Ltd
Paulton, Bristol. A member of BPCC plc
Macdonald & Co (Publishers) Ltd
Greater London House, Hampstead Road
London NW1 7QX. A BPCC plc company

RUPERT

and the Lonely Bird

Illustrated by Colin Petty
Based on an original story by Frederick Chaplain

Purnell

CHAPTER 1

One sunny morning Rupert was out for a stroll on Nutwood Common. As he approached the Girl Guides' hut, he suddenly heard Beryl the Guide calling her cat. She sounded worried, and anxious to know the reason, Rupert turned from his path and ran over to her.

"Hullo, Beryl. What's wrong with Dinkie?" he asked, seeing her puzzled frown. Dinkie was stalking away from her and her tail high in the air.

"Oh, hullo, Rupert," said Beryl. "I don't know what's wrong. I've just offered Dinkie a saucer of fresh milk, but she simply refused to drink it."

Knowing that it was unlike Dinkie to refuse milk, Rupert decided to follow the cat. Reassuring Beryl, he wandered on, and before long he came across Dinkie sitting on a milestone.

"Well, Dinkie," said the little bear, "tell me why you didn't want your milk just now."

"Puh!" sniffed Dinkie. "Why *would* I want it? I can get something much better than that now. I've found a friendly giant who gives me

a huge bowl of cream every morning. As a matter of fact he would like me to be his pet, and I'm seriously thinking of leaving home."

Rupert was very distressed to hear Dinkie's news. "Surely you wouldn't leave Beryl," he said in dismay. "She loves you—we *all* love you," he added, stroking the cat fondly.

"Oh, it's nice enough here," said Dinkie airily, "but the giant wants a pet so much, and if I lived with him I'd have cream every day. Beryl only gives me *milk*."

Rupert was just going to start persuading Dinkie to stay with her, when a sudden beating of wings caused the cat to start in alarm.

"Just look at that enormous bird!" she exclaimed in a fright. "I'm off!" And she bounded away, leaving Rupert to gaze at the great creature hovering nearby.

The bird was so very big that Rupert's first thought was to follow Dinkie and take to his heels, but as he paused for a second glance he murmured, "Oh, there's nothing to be afraid of. It's one of the carrier eagles from the Bird Kingdom."

So Rupert stood his ground and waited while the huge bird descended to a tree and placed something square in the branches.

"That's odd," thought Rupert. "It's a box—no, it's a *cage*. And there's something in it!"

The big bird spread its wings at this moment, but instead of flying away it circled round and round Rupert, who watched the creature uncertainly.

"Ooh, I think it's coming nearer," he gasped. Sure enough, the great bird approached Rupert and, finding a perch close by, thrust its beak close to the little bear.

"Ah, I was hoping to find you," it rasped.

"There is a task that I wish you to perform for our King. He commanded that the Dodo be brought to Nutwood. The King could find no rightful place for it at his palace, so he decided to send it to Nutwood, where it would be out of his way. I have left it in the tree over there. All that remains for you to do is to let it out of the cage and feed it each day."

Rupert had no time to question the eagle further before it spread its wings once more and took to the air.

"I wonder why I'm supposed to look after the Dodo?" mused Rupert. "I suppose it won't be very hard to let it out and feed it. But I simply must see what this strange creature looks like!"

With that the little bear set off over the grass to the tree where the cage had been set high in the branches.

CHAPTER 2

Rupert hurriedly began to climb the tree, and soon found the cage wedged firmly between some strong branches. "Oh dear, that's going to be far too big to move," murmured the little bear. "I shall have to open it here. I had no idea Dodos were so large." He noticed a bag dangling from the bottom of the cage.

"I suppose that's the Dodo's food," he muttered. He squirmed his way along one of the limbs of the tree until he was in a position to open the cage.

It was difficult to see much of the Dodo behind the bars, but the bird noticed Rupert straight away, and squawked: "So you've come to let me out, have you? And about time too!

As Rupert swung open the door of the cage, he got his first clear look at the Dodo. "Oooh, what a strange looking—" He checked himself, hurriedly, realising that the Dodo had overheard him.

"I—I d-didn't mean that," he faltered. "It's just that I've never seen one of you before."

"I should hope you didn't mean it," replied the Dodo, waddling from the cage. 'I'll have you know I'm the only one of my kind."

The ungainly bird perched on a branch and gazed about. "H'm, not much of a place for a bird of high rank," it croaked. "But it will do. I'll make the best of it."

While the Dodo was still taking in its new surroundings, Rupert

unfastened the food bag from the cage.

"W-welcome to Nutwood," he said, timidly. "The King of the Birds asked me to look after you. Aren't you hungry after your journey?"

"No, thank you," replied the Dodo. "Come back tomorrow with my meal."

Rupert was about to make his way down the tree, when he paused and asked: "Please, how long are you staying with us?"

"How long?" echoed the bird. "Why, for always, of course!"

Rupert was worried by this reply. He didn't see how he could feed the bird for ever, but as he descended the tree his thoughts were interrupted by the flapping of the Wise Owl, who was waiting anxiously below on a branch.

"What *is* that creaure you've let out of the cage?" he asked Rupert. "Why is it here?"

"It's a Dodo," explained Rupert. "Your King sent it here."

"A Dodo!" exclaimed the Wise Owl. "That's ridiculous! There's no such thing nowadays. I won't believe it! I'll take no notice of it and pretend it's not there."

When Rupert reached the ground the other birds fluttered towards him chirping. "Why must we have that bird in *our* wood?" they fussed. "Send it *away*!"

The Dodo caused such a stir among the other birds, and they were pestering Rupert with so many questions, that Rupert was glad to leave the wood. He hurried home, taking the bag of food with him, and as soon as he

arrived he made straight for Mr Bear's shed.

"I'll leave the Dodo's food in here," Rupert decided. "Mummy won't want it in the house."

He was very curious to see what the creature ate, so he shook out a little of the contents on to the floor. He was amazed to find nothing more than a few dry, thorny twigs.

"Is that all it lives on?' he gasped. Before he had time to wonder any more about the Dodo's diet, the little bear heard his Mummy calling to him urgently.

He rushed indoors, leaving the Dodo's food bag in the shed.

"I'm sorry to be so late, Mummy," he said. "Shall I tell you about the adventure I've had this morning?"

"Not now, dear," replied Mrs Bear. "I simply must get on with my housework."

She bustled off, leaving Rupert to his lunch. As he finished, he noticed smoke rising outside the window. Looking out he saw to his alarm that Mr Bear was

lighting a bonfire, and holding something in his hand which looked very much like the Dodo's food bag.

Rupert ran out of doors, shouting to his Daddy as he ran. "Don't, Daddy, don't!" he cried. 'That's the Dodo's food you're burning!"

Mr Bear stared at Rupert in bewilderment. "What *are* you talking about?" he said. "I found this bag of old cuttings in the shed, and I'm just getting rid of them."

"But that's the stuff the Dodo eats," explained Rupert, breathlessly. "Oh dear, the bag's empty! You've burned the lot, Daddy!"

The little bear was so upset that he made a

muddle of explaining why the bag of food was so important, and his Daddy was left feeling more confused than ever. At the cottage door Rupert stopped to ponder.

"Whatever am I going to do?" he murmured. "I haven't anything to feed the Dodo with now."

He was worried and miserable all evening, and seeing how upset he was Daddy tried to make amends for his mistake at bedtime.

"I'm still not quite clear why it was so

dreadfully wrong of me to burn those old twigs," he smiled. "Surely no bird would eat them. I've bought some birdseed for you to feed it instead. Why don't you try offering it some in the morning?"

Rupert thanked his father for his kind thought, and his Mummy and Daddy went out of the room and said goodnight.

CHAPTER 3

Left alone, Rupert switched on his bedside lamp and sat up in bed to think about the problem before him. "I do hope I can coax the Dodo to eat birdseed," he thought. Suddenly there was a tapping sound on the window, and Rupert peered in alarm. "There's a shadow moving about on the windowsill," he whispered. "Whatever can it be?"

Quietly he slipped out of bed and unfastened the window. There, perched on the sill, was the Wise Owl, wide-eyed and ruffled.

"It's no use," he cried. "We can't stand it! Besides, it snores!"

"W-what snores?" asked Rupert in surprise.

"That awful Dodo," retorted the Owl. "Stays in *my* tree all the time and refuses to move. Now the other birds are too scared to come and ask my advice. And you should hear the noise it makes when it's asleep! You'll just *have* to find another home for it. Goodnight!" And with that, the Wise Owl glided away into the darkness.

The next morning Rupert told his Mummy of the Wise Owl's visit. "Please may I go out early this morning, to feed the Dodo?" he asked.

"Yes, of course," replied Mrs Bear. "But are you sure about its name? Daddy seems to think it can't possibily be a Dodo."

"Oh, but it is, Mummy," insisted Rupert. "It's the only one of its kind."

Carefully carrying the box of birdseed, Rupert was hurrying across the Common next morning, when Dinkie the cat darted from a hedge. "Just a moment, Rupert," purred the little cat. "I've something rather important to tell you. I've had second thoughts about leaving home. I've decided to stay with Beryl after all."

Rupert was overjoyed at Dinkie's news, and kneeling beside the cat he stroked her head.

"Oh, Dinkie, that's splendid," he said. "And you know, you've given me an idea. I've been told to find another home for a big bird. Do you think the giant would like it for a pet instead of you?"

"What a good idea," mewed Dinkie. "I think the giant might be very pleased. I'll go at once and ask him. It will take me some time to get there and back, but please wait for me by the old windmill on the downs."

Dinkie bounded merrily away on her long journey to the friendly giant. Rupert watched until the cat was out of sight. "I do believe everything will turn out right after all," he said to himself. "Everyone will be happy. If the Dodo becomes the giant's pet it won't bother the Wise Owl any more. And the other birds will be happy too."

He turned towards the wood, but he had not gone far before a whole family of birds swooped down and flew around him.

"Have you come to feed that creature?" they screeched. "We want him to go! Take him away from here!"

More and more birds began to gather round Rupert chorusing angrily, and the little bear was forced to run for shelter to the Wise Owl's tree. Anxiously he called the Dodo. The ungainly creature clambered down, and Rupert sprinkled his birdseed on a rock for him.

"I'm awfully sorry it isn't your proper food," he explained nervously, "but those twigs were burnt by mistake on my Daddy's bonfire."

"Humph, and you expect me to eat this stuff?" grunted the Dodo. "I'd rather go without."

The other birds, who had been circling around the pair, overheard this, and fluttered round with chirrups of delight. "There's nothing for it to eat," they tittered. "Now it will *have* to go."

The noise at last became too much for Rupert. "Stop!" he shouted. "You're all being silly! I've got something to tell the Dodo. Will you please keep quiet!"

He quickly told the great creature of Dinkie's journey to the giant, to ask him if he would like the Dodo for a pet.

"A giant, eh?" remarked the Dodo, with a chuckle. "Yes, I'm sure I would be happy with him."

With a sigh of relief, Rupert led the Dodo out of the wood. Once outside they were left in peace.

"I arranged to meet Dinkie by the old windmill," he explained. "It's not far from here."

At last they reached the meeting place on the downs, but as Rupert scanned the horizon he could see no sign of the cat.

"We must be patient, and wait," he told the Dodo. "Dinkie said it would take her a long while to get there and back."

CHAPTER 4

Time went by and Rupert and the Dodo were still sitting patiently beside the windmill. The Dodo had even fallen asleep and was snoring gently.

Suddenly Rupert spied a dark shape streaking across the fields.

"Here she is," he cried excitedly. The Dodo woke with a start and shook his head. "About time too," he grunted, but despite his gruff tone, he looked very hopeful.

Rupert dashed to meet Dinkie, and the Dodo lumbered along behind him. "Hullo, Dinkie," said Rupert breathlessly. "What did the giant say?"

"Whew! I'm completely out of breath,"

panted the cat. "But it's all fixed. The giant likes the idea of a pet Dodo. He thanked you for your kind thought and asked if you would be good enough to take the Dodo there today."

"Where does the giant live?" asked Rupert. "And how long will it take to get there?" he added.

"Well," said Dinkie, "I'm a very fast runner, as you know, but if you walk it will take hours and hours. Mind you, you can't miss the giant's home if you make sure you keep your face to the breeze. He lives in a cave at the foot of a hill."

"That's all I need to know," chimed in the Dodo. "Cats aren't the only creatures who can run. I'll carry the little bear."

Rupert turned in surprise, but as soon as he

climbed up and perched on the Dodo's back, it set off at such an amazing pace that he was glad they weren't walking. He clung to the creature's neck as it sped along at top speed, and he was soon carried away from Nutwood and across lonely parts he had never seen before. At long last a range of rocks came into view, and the Dodo slowed down. "This must be the place we're looking for," it panted. "Dinkie said nothing about climbing rocks, and we'd certainly have to do that if we went any further."

Rupert gazed at the smooth rocks. "I can't see any sign of a cave," he murmured. "I'd better go and explore."

He slipped from the Dodo's back, and leaving it to regain its breath he made his way

along the foot of the rocks, which appeared to lead up into steep cliffs.

Suddenly he noticed a cleft. Shouting to the Dodo, he pointed it out.

"Look, that may be the giant's cave!" he exclaimed. "Stay there and I'll take a closer look."

Cautiously Rupert neared the cleft. He felt a little bit nervous now. "I wonder how big that giant is," he mused. "Of course he may just be a tall man. He would seem like a giant to Dinkie."

Then he noticed some steps leading to the opening. "My, they're enormous!" he gasped.

There didn't seem to be any sound or movement inside the cave, so, mustering his courage, Rupert crept nearer the opening and peered into the gloom.

Suddenly a great arm reached out and picked up the little bear between finger and thumb.

"Ho, ho, ho! What's this I see?" said a deep voice.

Rupert flinched at the hearty bellow, but, unhurt, he was placed in the palm of a massive hand. Rupert looked up nervously to see a huge face with a big friendly grin spreading across it. It was the giant himself, and a truly enormous man he was.

"So," he chuckled, "you're my new pet! You must be the Dodo."

"P-please, I'm not the Dodo," said Rupert, trembling in the palm of the giant's hand. He scrambled to his feet so that the giant could see him better. "The Dodo's a big bird," he explained. "I left it outside while I came to find you."

The great man seemed good natured enough. "Ah, pray forgive me," he said, gently placing Rupert on the floor of the cave. "May I see my new pet? I promised I will wait here and stay still, in case my size should scare it away."

Thankful to find the giant so friendly, Rupert went off to call the Dodo.

"Come and meet your new master," he called. "I've spoken to him and he's waiting here to see you."

CHAPTER 5

The Dodo roused himself from another forty winks and Rupert led him into the cave.

The giant beamed with pleasure and clapped his hands. "What a magnificent bird!" he exclaimed. "I could wish for no better creature. And just the right size to perch on my shoulder, too. Ah, how happy I am to have a pet of my own at last."

The Dodo fluffed up its feathers and smiled at its new owner. While the two were busy making friends, Rupert glanced around the cave and noticed a huge bowl filled with dry, thorny twigs.

"Why, surely this is Dodo-food!" he murmured in surprise.

He picked up the twigs and carried them over to the giant.

"I say," he said. "I am sure this is the same sort of stuff that the Dodo eats. Now I shan't need to worry about getting food for it."

The giant looked amused. "Aye," he said "Those twigs are plentiful in these parts. Indeed, I often eat them myself. I find them very tasty and tender when they're boiled. Why don't we let the Dodo try them?"

The Dodo was more than ready to try some of its favourite food, and was already hopping impatiently from one foot to the other. Smiling at its antics, the giant offered the creature some twigs, and was delighted when it pecked eagerly at them.

"Absolutely delicious," croaked the Dodo. "It's a long time since I had a decent meal!"

Rupert hastily explained about his Daddy's bonfire, and the giant smiled and nodded at the little bear's story. Rupert also told him about the unfriendly birds in the wood, and the giant promised that he would not take the Dodo anywhere near it.

The giant watched fondly as the strange bird gobbled hungrily at the twigs.

"Eat up, my precious pet," he said. "You shall have as much of that food as you want. We will go out together this evening and find some more."

Rupert was waiting patiently nearby, wondering how he was going to get home in time for tea. He seemed to have been away for a very long time and was getting hungry.

As if he read Rupert's thoughts, the giant turned to him and said, "What about your journey back, my little friend? No doubt you have a long way to go, and your legs are short. I will see what I can do to get you home swiftly."

He pointed to a food bowl which was full of large, round biscuits.

"First bring me four of those," he said, smiling at the little bear.

Rupert picked up one of the biscuits. "Ooh—they're just like wheels," he laughed. "I wonder what's in store for me now!"

CHAPTER 6

Rupert setled down to watch the giant, and was immediately put on the table so that he had a better view.

The giant set to work, first boring a hole in each hard, round biscuit. Then he found a short length of log and lashed two wooden axles to it.

"This is just like a toy to me," he laughed. "But it will be quite large enough for you to ride upon, my tiny friend."

"I only wish I knew what you were making," said Rupert with a smile. "It all looks very exciting!" Rupert watched intently.

The giant kept silent. He was enjoying this guessing game with his new little friend.

At last the biscuit wheels were firmly fixed, and the giant quickly added a slender mast to the log. "Oooh! I can guess now," cried Rupert. "What a clever idea. I know what you are making; it's a sail-car—a boat that can travel on dry land—isn't it?

The giant chuckled good-naturedly. "You are correct, little bear," he said.

Rupert was jumping up and down with excitement at the prospect of driving his very own sail-car, and impatient to try it out, he helped the giant fasten the three-cornered sail to the mast.

"There, it's ready now," said the giant, standing back to look at his handiwork. "Although I say it myself, it *is* rather a nice little car; one of the best I've made, in fact. Just try it to see if it's the right size for you."

Rupert clambered on

to the log and sat astride it. "Oh, yes, it's fine," he said. "And I can steer with the sail rope. This is going to be fun, and it will be so much quicker than walking all that way home. Thank you, thank you!"

The giant beamed with pleasure. "I like making toys," he said, "and with a little help from me you will have a swift journey home.

It's but a small reward for bringing me this lovely bird."

With the Dodo on his shoulder, he carried Rupert in one hand and the wheeled boat in the other, and they went outside the cave.

All that remained for Rupert was to say goodbye to the Dodo. "The giant is very kind," he said. "You'll like being his pet."

"Yes, I shall be very happy here," agreed the Dodo. "It's an honour to belong to a giant."

As soon as Rupert had settled himself astride the sail-car the giant began his instructions. "You'll have to keep a very tight hold on the rope at first, my little friend, otherwise you may be blown off course."

Then he lay flat on the ground and, taking a deep breath, gave an enormous puff.

The sail billowed out, and the little car was thrown forward with such force that Rupert was almost thrown off balance. A cloud of dust swirled round him as he tried to control the speeding sail-car.

"I can't see which way I'm going," he gasped. "I do hope I won't bump into anything!"

Suddenly he emerged from the cloud of dust and, leaving it floating behind him, he saw a clear course ahead. Glancing back, he could see his huge friend waving farewell above the dust, with the Dodo watching from his shoulder.

"This is fine," he thought. "I'll be home in no time at all!"

CHAPTER 7

All the way across high ground the breeze kept Rupert's sail-car rolling along, and at last he reached the downhill stretch to Nutwood.

"Hooray, I'm back!" he cried, as he saw the Conjurer's tall house standing out above the treetops.

In the valley there was less wind, but the sail-car had enough speed to take it as far as Nutwood Farm before it finally came to a halt.

"There's Dinkie the cat!" exclaimed the little bear, noticing a small dark shape among the farm buildings. "I must go and tell her about my adventure."

Rupert jumped off his sail-car and ran towards the cat. Then, to his surprise, Beryl appeared from the farmhouse, carrying a jug, and Dinkie sidled fondly around her.

"Hullo, Rupert, where have you come from?" said the Guide. "I didn't see you on my way to the farm. I came here to get a little cream as a treat for Dinkie," she added, "and the farmer had so much to spare that he gave me this whole jugful. It's Dinkie's lucky day!"

"So that's why she's looking so pleased with herself," smiled Rupert.

He was delighted that Beryl had managed to get her cat such a lovely treat. "It's come at just the right time," he thought.

Beryl stared at the sail-car. "Whatever is that clumsy thing?" she asked.

"It's a sail-car," laughed Rupert. "Do you know, I've had the most exciting time . . ."

"Ooh, do tell me about it, Rupert," said Beryl excitedly. "You do have such wonderful adventures."

"It's a long story," began Rupert, and he told her the whole story.

"Well," he said, as he finished, "if you Guides will ask the Scouts to look after the sail-car for me, they can use it whenever they like. Now I must hurry home, or I'll be late." Beryl promised she would pass on Rupert's message to the Scouts.

As the friends separated, Dinkie hovered beside Rupert.

"You won't tell Beryl I was thinking of leaving home, will you?" she whispered anxiously.

"I won't breathe a word of it," promised Rupert. "Look Beryl's waiting for you. Go and enjoy that jug of cream, you lucky puss!"